Kathy Roth
116F Erickson Hall
517-349-5811
rothk@msu.edu

W9-ABY-946

THE GREAT POTATO BOOK

by Meredith Sayles Hughes and E. Thomas Hughes
drawings by G. Brian Karas

Macmillan Publishing Company
New York
Collier Macmillan Publishers
London

Macmillan Publishing Company
866 Third Avenue, New York, NY 10022
Collier Macmillan Canada, Inc.
First Edition
Printed in the United States of America
10   9   8   7   6   5   4   3   2   1
The photographs on pages 43, 45, 47, and 49 are included courtesy
of The New York Public Library Picture Collection; all other
photographs, courtesy of The Potato Museum, Washington, D.C.
The story on pages 18–19 is used by permission of the author.
The jokes on page 73 appear in *Potato Jokes,* copyright © 1984 by
Paul McMahon, and are reprinted by permission of Pocket Books,
a division of Simon & Schuster, Inc.
The text of this book is set in 16 pt. Garamond No. 3.
The drawings are rendered in pen-and-ink.
Library of Congress Cataloging-in-Publication Data
Hughes, Meredith.
The great potato book.
Summary: Discusses many aspects of the nutritious,
delicious, versatile potato—its history, usefulness,
and folklore, with games, jokes, and rhymes.
1. Potatoes—Juvenile literature.   2. Potato
products—Juvenile literature.   3. Potatoes—Folklore—
Juvenile literature.   4. Games—Juvenile literature.
{1. Potatoes}   I. Hughes, Thomas, date.
II. Karas, Brian, ill.   III. Title.
SB211.P8H77   1986   641.3′521   85-24033
ISBN 0-02-745300-6

To our parents

We are grateful to Judith Kohlhaas, who had the idea for this book. We're thankful for Christian Kohlhaas and Gulliver Hughes, even though their arrival on the scene considerably interrupted and delayed completion of our tuber tome.

Contents

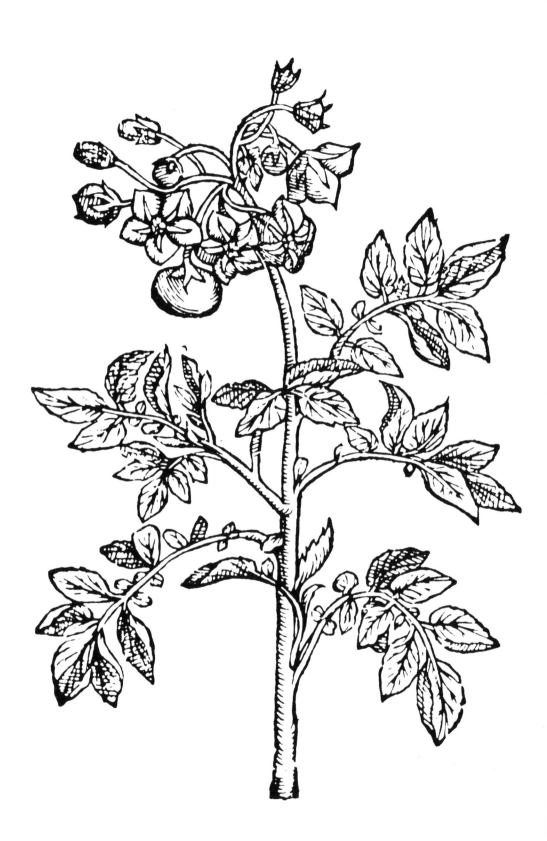

THE LIVING POTATO

What Is a Potato?

Take a potato in your hand. You are holding the world's most important vegetable. Potatoes produce more pounds of protein per acre than corn, rice, wheat, or oats.

When you eat French fries or mashed potatoes, you are not alone. All around the world people rich and poor are eating the same thing, enjoying the same friendly taste, benefiting from the same considerable nutrition. The goodness of the potato knows no bounds.

Why is the potato so important? Because it is as perfect as any one food can be: packed with nutrients, low in fat, generous in bulk, delicious

This early portrait of the potato appeared in Charles de l'Écluse's book *Historia* in 1629.

in taste, versatile in preparation, and protectively packaged for transport and long storage. Nothing need be wasted in the potato, not even the water it is cooked in.

Take a closer look at the potato in your hand. You know it has eyes. Find them. Notice the eyebrows over each one. All the eyebrows look in the same direction, toward the eye end of the potato, so called because there are more eyes clustered together there. The other end of your potato should show traces of a stem, the place where the *tuber* (as the potato is called) was attached to the main plant system.

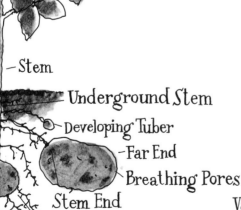

Fruit (formed from Flower)

Flower

End leaflet

Stem

Underground Stem

Developing Tuber

Far End

Breathing Pores

Eye

Stem End

Old "Seed" Potato

True Roots

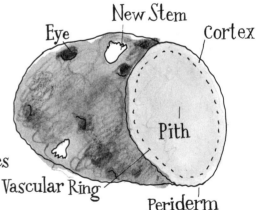

New Stem

Eye

Cortex

Pith

Vascular Ring

Periderm

The potato, like any of the rest of us, has a top and a bottom, even a front and a back. When you plant a potato, you plant it with the eye end up and the stem end down, covered with about two inches of soil. From the eyes come buds, which grow into stocky sprouts.

Up close, the sprouts look like hairy visitors from another planet. The sprouts grow tall and green aboveground.

Potatoes are not roots at all, but storage areas, part of the plant's underground stem. Under the soil the potato plant sends out roots, which search the ground for water and food the growing plant needs. The roots find much more food than the plant can use at one time. So the plant stores the excess food in clever oval packages called tubers. These are the potatoes we know and love.

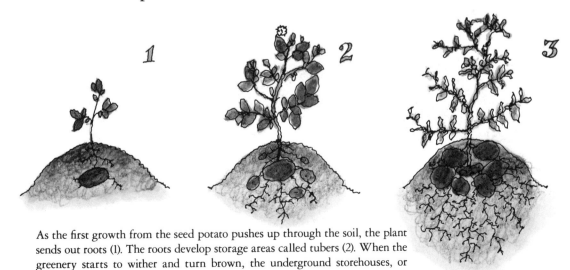

As the first growth from the seed potato pushes up through the soil, the plant sends out roots (1). The roots develop storage areas called tubers (2). When the greenery starts to wither and turn brown, the underground storehouses, or potatoes, are ready for harvest (3).

The Potato Has a Family, Too

Each of us comes from a family, and so does the potato. Its official family name is Solanaceae. Scientists use a Latin word to describe a group of plants that share certain family characteristics, such as similar-looking leaves and flowers. The potato's own formal name is *Solanum tuberosum.*

The tomato is one of the potato's relatives. It has sturdy green stems and leaves and five-sided, star-shaped flowers like the potato. Compare the tomato to the potato when both plants are in bloom. They do look like cousins, at least. Other plants we like to eat are also related to the potato: the chili pepper and the eggplant.

Tomato   chili Pepper   Eggplant   Red Pontiac Potato   Petunia

Then there are those we had best not eat, the poisonous nightshade and belladonna. We plant another relative, the petunia, in flower beds. And finally, there is the tobacco plant, a source of material for chewing and puffing. The potato was originally found in South America. All these plants are American cousins, descendants of parents born here eons ago.

What Variety!

You can grow as many as 10,000 different kinds of potatoes at home, if you have the room. Some will be pink, some almost white, some close to purple, some tan. Some will have white flesh, some yellow, some lavender. Each will taste a bit different from the others. Each will have a slightly different feel and look to it.

If you had the time and patience to try them

Nightshade   Tobacco   Belladonna

all, you would soon discover that some were better for boiling, some for baking, and some for frying. There are even potatoes available today that are not intended for eating at all. They are grown especially for use in industry.

The starch in the potato is extracted and used in candy making to hold the candy together. It is also used in the making of instant soups.

Potatoes haven't always been good-looking and good-tasting. The ones first eaten by Europeans in the 1530s were tiny, knobby, and odd-tasting. But the people who grew them began to select tubers from the plants that had given the best product. These they replanted the following season, and the plants produced more good potatoes. The Italians in particular may have done the most to improve the *spud* (a nickname for the potato) in the early days.

Selective planting was just one way to grow better potatoes. Today plant scientists combine characteristics from several plants to produce a

specific potato for a specific purpose, such as a
potato that can withstand an early frost. Then
farmers who work in colder regions can plant the
potato that will bring them the best results.

The Colorado Potato Beetle

Born in the vast plains of the American West,
the Colorado potato beetle originally dined on the
leaves of wild members of the potato family—
that is, until it developed a taste for the garden
potatoes brought from the East by the settlers.
The beetles soon left their weed-eating days behind and have since hopped, skipped, and flown
after the cultivated potato throughout much of
the world.

The beetle is destructive because it devours all
the leaves of a potato plant. The plant struggles
to stay alive, putting little energy into producing
potatoes.

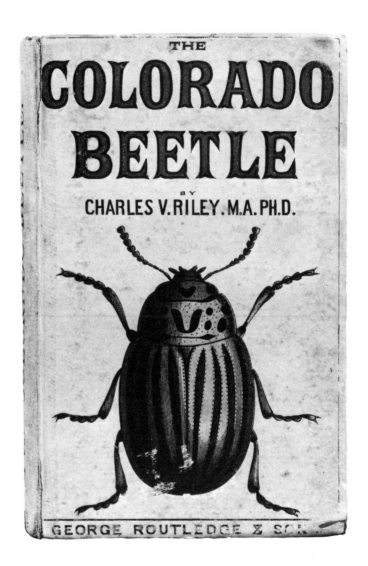

The beetle story was told in this little book
published in 1877.

So the world has fought back, trying to wipe
out the insect with powders and sprays and bitter
chemicals. The battle is expensive and the beetle,
like others of its kind, seems to be getting used
to the powders and sprays.

The beetle does have some natural enemies,
and many young beetles are gobbled up by larger
insects and by birds. The bobwhite and the rose-
breasted grosbeak in particular seem to fancy the
Colorado beetle for lunch.

Have a Hairy Pet Potato

Choose a large potato. Give it a good face. You
can draw one with a felt-tip marker or carve out
a face with a knife or stick interesting things into
the potato, such as cloves for eyes.

The hairy part comes next. Carve out a hunk
from the top of the potato, as if you were remov-
ing the top of a pumpkin. Fill the cavity with

moistened cotton. Slice off the bottom of the potato and set it in a dish of water in a sunny spot. Sprinkle grass or bird seed on the cotton and water it every day. Your pet potato will soon be bald no more.

Plant a Potato to Get a Potato

That's right. Generally speaking we plant specially grown small spuds known as "seed potatoes" in our gardens and on our farms. Sometimes the seed potato is large and it is cut into smaller pieces, each containing an eye, and then planted.

The potato plant can produce true seed from

the fruit that grows where the flower once
bloomed, but the fruit doesn't always form.

The seed potatoes you buy for your garden have been developed by plant scientists and grown under ideal conditions.

Grow Your Own Potatoes

Start with a clay pot and put in a few handfuls of moist potting soil. Plant the potato, eye end up, in the soil. Cover the potato with more soil until the pot is half full. Place it in a sunny spot, water when dry, and when the shoots come up, add more soil. Be sure to stake up the plants when they grow tall.

After about six or eight weeks, harvest your

potatoes by gently knocking the plant out of the pot and onto an old newspaper. You should have a handful of tiny spuds.

You can grow a bigger crop in a trash can. Place four seed potatoes on a six-inch layer of earth in the bottom of the can. Cover with about four inches of soil. Allow the shoots to grow about four inches tall and then add two more inches of soil. Keep adding soil until you run out of trash can. Water the soil, but don't let it get soggy. When the stalks turn brown and wither, dig down and lift up your potatoes.

Did You Know . .

. . that potatoes were first grown in North America in 1621, in Virginia?

. . that the potato is the only vegetable that grows in the desert as well as in mountains above 14,000 feet?

. . that in 1974 an Englishman named Eric Jenkins grew 370 pounds of potatoes from one plant?

THE POWERFUL POTATO

Food is fuel for our bodies. We eat in order to give ourselves strength. We would come to a halt if we stopped eating, just as a car that has run out of gas stops rolling. If we imagined our bodies as engines and food as fuel, we might be more sensible about what we eat.

Potatoes are powerful body fuel. If you ate nothing but potatoes and milk you would be healthy and strong. But you would probably be tired of potatoes! You would be eating at least twelve potatoes a day. And you might lose a little weight at the same time. You would certainly not gain any weight.

Potatoes provide fuel for more than people and animals. Broken down into alcohol they can be

Potato alcohol fueled this nineteenth-century German street lamp.

16   used to run machines, large and small. Gasohol, a mixture of gasoline and ethanol (potato alcohol is a form of ethanol), made from old or surplus potatoes, powers tractors and trucks on farms. At the turn of the century Germans were using this fuel in stoves, lamps, and even irons for pressing clothes.

If you had lived in England during World War I, you might have sent a friend a postcard like this one. Potatoes were in short supply and people missed their favorite vegetable.

But you don't always need to convert the potato to alcohol in order to get energy for powering machines. You can actually tap the potato itself and produce electricity.

A man in North Carolina has invented what he calls a Tater Time Clock. It's a digital-display clock that has no batteries and no outside source of power. It runs on potatoes—two of them.

The spuds are put on the ends of two rods that stick out from the clock casing, one zinc and one copper. The metal reacts with the acids inside the potato to create a current sufficient to run the clock.

The clock's inventor says he changes the potatoes every four weeks, not because the spuds have lost their strength, but because they've begun to smell.

Survival Spuds

A nine-year-old girl and her mother living in Poland were forced to leave their home during World War II and walk toward the border to safety. They traveled lightly, moving only at night and avoiding the large cities. They ran out of food after a few days. They were forced to stop at village houses, offering to work in exchange for food.

"In return for labor, we were given a few potatoes—raw, often pitted, but still food. With a penknife, my mother would scrape off the dirt, then slice it [one potato] thin, place it on the stove till the edges curled and turned to charcoal. And then we ate. And then we lived. . . . We had no fats, nothing to heat or fry it in—it was the potato and the fire.

"More often, we would find ourselves without shelter, and then we would forage in the potato fields, in case some potatoes had not been dug up. Without the potato we might have died along the route."

The little girl, Masha Leon, and her mother survived. They rejoined Masha's father and eventually came to the United States to live.

In World War II, dancing, smiling Potato Pete urged the English to plant potatoes instead of flowers or green grass around their homes. Wheat and other grains were scarce and only potatoes could be eaten without elaborate processing. Pete was created by the Ministry of Food and appeared on many posters throughout the war.

Potato Diets

A diet is simply a selection of food. Your diet is what you eat every day. More than one food expert through the years has recommended that we eat more potatoes.

In 1895 a Danish doctor named Mikkel Hindhede went on a potatoes and strawberries diet. He ate the potatoes with a bit of margarine. Not certain his experiment would succeed, the doctor waited to see what would happen.

Nothing happened. He felt fine. He continued to investigate the value of the potato in diet. Several years later his assistant, Frederick Madsen, went on a full six-month spud diet. In June 1931 a newspaper sponsored a bicycle race between Madsen and the owner of a Copenhagen butcher-shop chain. They agreed to race a distance of 55 kilometers. The butcher won the race by only two seconds, so clearly potato power had held its own.

These people were testing the power of the potato. They were not intent on losing weight. But for potato lovers who are, there are several different spud diets to choose from.

A Tucson, Arizona, man celebrating his hundredth birthday said he attributed his long life to a habit of including potatoes in his diet every day.

An eighty-year-old New Jersey man runs in marathons. He is also convinced his health and vigor come from a steady supply of spuds.

The earliest reference to the long lives of potato eaters comes from a man named Francisco Lopez de Gomara, who was with the Spanish conquistadors in Peru in 1552. He wrote about people who lived for one hundred years or more. "They lack maize [corn] and eat certain roots similar to truffles which they call *papas*." Potatoes again.

Potatoes are good for you. They fill you and give you the energy you need. When you eat potatoes you don't crave things that aren't good for you, such as candy and sugary soft drinks.

Did You Know . . that mashed potatoes are sometimes fed to poorly nourished babies when they can eat nothing else? The babies usually recover their health.

Dogs, cats, and rabbits like mashed potatoes, too — just be sure the potatoes are not too runny.

Feed Your Animal Friends

One hundred years ago this recipe for chicken feed appeared in an agricultural newspaper.

"A cheap and nutritious breakfast for fowls may be made by mixing meal with warm water to the consistency of paste, and stirring in potatoes with their skins, boiled and mashed. Potato parings, which are generally thrown away, should be boiled for fowls, who eat them with avidity."

Avidity is not another name for sugar. It means the chickens eat their potato food eagerly. Naturally. They are eating all the potato, even the skins.

THE DELICIOUS POTATO

The Potato Chip

Since the average person in the United States eats about four pounds of potato chips a year, we might as well know what we're eating.

Chips are thin slices of fresh potato fried quickly in hot vegetable oil. Originally potato chips were served hot as a vegetable side dish.

In the United States the story goes that in the 1850s George Crum, a chef at a restaurant on Saratoga Lake in New York, first served them up hot to some fussy customers who complained that his fried potatoes were too thick. (He may or may not have cut them with his own razor!) The next day Crum's potato chips appeared on all the tables

Chips were scooped out of containers and put into paper packets in the 1940s and 1950s.

of the restaurant in little baskets. Soon people were selling chips in paper packets at the Saratoga race track. The potatoes became known as Saratoga chips.

A man in Massachusetts began selling them to people who were going to the beach. Eventually potato chips were sold in stores from counter-top containers full of loose chips, the way penny candies were sold. Finally one or two companies started to cook, package, and distribute chips under their own brand names.

Today these "portable potatoes" are eaten by people all over the world.

(In England chips are "crisps" and French fries are "chips.")

Wooden slicers for potato chips

Years ago, you could order potato chips delivered to the door in tins like these.

The French Fry

People have been frying hunks or slices of potatoes in oil ever since there have been potatoes and
oil. But the fries eaten today by the millions were
probably born in the countries of Holland, Belgium, and France.

Tradition has it that Thomas Jefferson, third
president of the United States, brought a recipe
for fries back from France in 1802 and served the
potatoes at the White House.

Much later, the American soldiers stationed in
northern France and Belgium during World War
I loved the local potato specialty. They called the

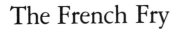

European French-fry cutter

spuds "French fries" because the people selling them spoke French.

The classic French fry is crispy on the outside and mealy on the inside because it is fried twice, the first time at 450° Fahrenheit. The fries are then allowed to drain and cool. Just before serving they are refried at 375°, drained, lightly salted, and served. Some cooks don't worry about exact temperatures. Instead, they toss a cube of bread into the hot oil. If the bread looks golden and crisp after only a five-second dunking, the oil is ready for the potatoes.

If You Prefer a Baked Potato

Fries used to be the only spuds served in fast-food restaurants. But today you can easily find a quick meal of baked potatoes with toppings. The potatoes are cooked in microwave or other high-speed ovens so that the customer gets a freshly baked, piping-hot spud.

Logo for a jazz club in North Hollywood, California

The choices of topping are endless, but according to surveys the most frequently chosen combination is butter, grated cheese, and sour cream. There are well over two hundred baked-potato shops in the United States.

Baked potatoes as quick meals are not new. In Victorian England the baked potato seller was a familiar figure on city street corners. He baked his spuds over hot coals in a portable oven. An inexpensive meal in a peel, the street baked potato was also useful as a hand warmer. Ladies of the time used to carry them in their muffs.

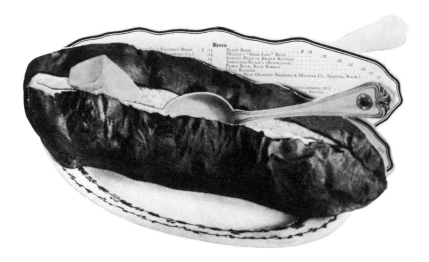

The Northern Pacific Railroad ran from St. Paul, Minnesota, to Seattle, Washington—the route of the Great Big Baked Potato, as they called it. This dining car menu from 1915 looks good enough to eat.

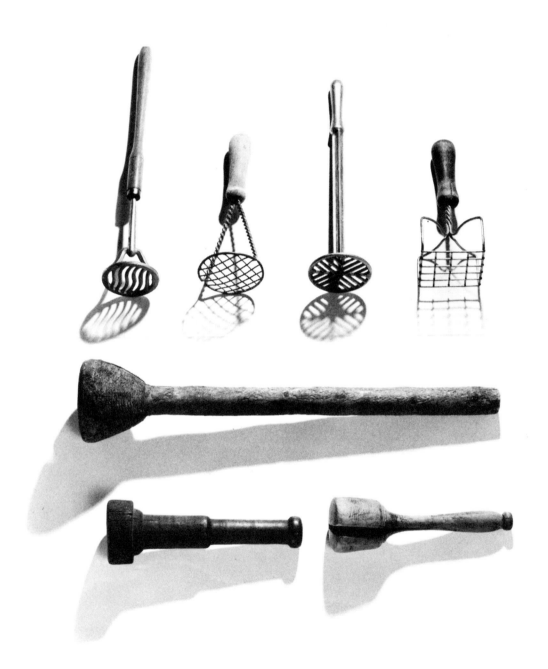

How to Make Delicious Mashies

Put a pot of water on the stove to boil. Select firm, healthy potatoes. Scrub but don't peel them. Cut them up in hunks of about equal size. Give the hunks a quick rinse to remove any dirt. When the water boils, carefully slide in the potatoes. Boil until the spuds are tender to the touch of a fork, but not mushy. Drain off the cooking water and save it. Add a bit of milk and a pat of butter. Mash. You can use a fork, the back of a large spoon, or a potato masher. Add some of the potato water you've drained off. Mash again. Keep adding milk or potato water until your mashies are the way you like them. Some people like them on the dry side, others smooth and creamy. If you like, add a tiny pinch of salt and eat them with butter on top.

The water the potatoes have cooked in is worth using again because it's full of vitamins. Use it in

Mashers come in a pleasing variety of shapes.

soup or drink it straight. (There are drinks that taste better, we must admit.) But be sure to put what you don't use in the refrigerator, and cook with it the next day.

Nothing in the potato needs to go to waste.

"Little pigs eat great potatoes."—Irish saying

The first published recipe for potatoes appeared in Germany in 1581. *"Boil diced potatoes, roast them in bacon fat and simmer the result in milk."*
—Ein Neues Kochbuch
Markus Rumpolt

Feed the Birds

Melt 2 ounces of fat or suet with 8 ounces of flour and 2 ounces of grated raw potato. Let cool and form into an oblong shape while not yet firm. Tie up with string like a package and hang out for the birds.

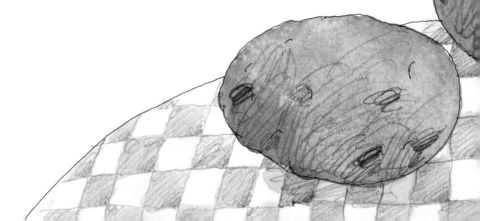

Did You Know . . that the word *pothole* refers to the hole made in the dirt floor of an Irish cottage? Each day potatoes were boiled in a heavy iron pot. The pot was removed from the fire and set in a shallow hole in the ground to keep it steady. The potatoes were mashed directly in the pot with a wood or iron masher. The repeated blows of the masher pushed the pot farther into the earth. As the pot was always put in the same place near the hearth, a sizeable pothole soon developed.

HOME SWEET HOME

THE VALUABLE POTATO

You don't usually expect a vegetable to do more than provide food for people or animals. And the potato in fact supplies food for both. But this terrific vegetable also contributes ingredients essential for making things such as plastics, medicines, paper, cloth, many types of glue, and candies. Oil-well drillers use a potato product that keeps their drills dry enough to maintain the required friction.

The potato is deemed to have worth beyond what it gives us in raw material. It is the only vegetable that is traded, like stocks or bonds of a corporation, on a financial exchange.

The island people of Tristan da Cunha used potatoes instead of money. Potatoes were their major source of wealth, their prime food supply. This potato stamp dates from 1946. The British-owned island is halfway between Africa and South America.

The potato provides a livelihood to thousands of people: to scientists who develop new varieties; to farmers and their employees who grow them; to dealers who buy and then sell them to processing plants that make other food and industrial products from them, or to supermarkets, which in turn sell them directly to you and me. Then there are the truckers who transport them, the packers who pack them, even the people who design and produce the sacks, bags, boxes, and barrels potatoes come in. Potato people are everywhere.

The Military Potato

Though calm and unaggressive itself, the potato has proved a formidable weapon to those who engage in war. It has fed the people who fought, as well as those who stayed behind. It can wait patiently, hidden underground until it is needed. It can be added to other food such as wheat to make powerful bread. It is not easily destroyed.

It was even turned into fuel during World War II to power rockets and army trucks for the Germans.

The Cure-It-All Potato

Regular potato-eaters probably won't ever need to try any of these old-time folk remedies for minor ailments because they are so healthy. But, just in case, here they are—all-potato cures people have found effective and told their families and friends about through the centuries. To keep yourself healthy, try potatoes on the outside as well as on the inside.

FOR FACIAL BLEMISHES:
Wash face daily with cool potato juice.

FOR SUNBURN:
Apply raw grated potato or juice to red areas. Do the same for frostbite.

. . that in times of hardship, workers have frequently accepted potatoes instead of money?

. . that on the South Atlantic island of Tristan da Cunha, potatoes were once used as the country's unofficial currency instead of money?

. . that Colorado miners of the 1840s planted potatoes along the creeks where they panned for gold?

. . that during the Alaskan Klondike gold rush, potatoes were worth almost their weight in gold?

. . that those who purchased food for Queen Elizabeth I's table in England in 1590 bought then-rare potatoes for an "enormous" price?

FOR TOOTHACHE :

Carry a potato in your pocket.

FOR SORE THROAT :

Put a slice of baked potato in a stocking and tie it around your neck.

FOR ACHES AND PAINS:

Rub the area with the water potatoes have been boiled in.

THE WELL-TRAVELED POTATO

1000 B.C.
Andean Indian

Mountain Indians living in what is now Peru first gathered wild potatoes; later they planted, harvested, and stored them. They removed the moisture from the potatoes by leaving them out on the ground overnight to freeze. The next day the potatoes would thaw in the sun, bursting the expanded cells. Water could then be squeezed out of the tubers. The Incas kept them dried, or *dehydrated*, until needed.

1550
Spanish explorer

These *conquistadores,* or conquerors, looking for gold in South America ran out of their own food and had to eat what the natives were eating, *patatas.* One of them put potatoes in the hold of a ship that was returning to Spain.

1570
Spanish gardener

A curious food-lover in Spain planted potatoes that had been brought on a ship returning from South America. Very soon, a hospital in Seville was feeding potatoes to its patients. This is the earliest verified appearance of the potato in the Old World.

S.ᵗ *FRANCIS DRAKE*.

1586
Sir Francis Drake

After sacking the city Cartagena in South America, Drake filled the hold of his ship with the spoils of conquest, including potatoes. On his way home, he stopped at Roanoke, in Virginia, to pick up people who wanted to return to England. Among his passengers was Thomas Hariot, a naturalist, one of Sir Walter Raleigh's men. Drake's samples of spuds ultimately became known as "Virginia potatoes," which they were not, and Raleigh's name became linked with the discovery, though he had nothing to do with it. Drake was responsible for introducing the potato to northern Europe.

1597
John Gerard

1601
Charles de l'Écluse or Clusius

This English gardener wrote and published in London the first description of the potato in English. He was so impressed by the New World vegetable that he held a sprig of a flowering plant in his hand as he sat for his portrait.

A botanist (a person who professionally studies plants) living in what is today Belgium popularized the potato by spreading the word about it among other learned people of the time.

44

1621
Capt. Nathaniel Butler, Governor of Bermuda

The first potatoes arrived in North America when Captain Butler sent two large cedar chests containing potatoes and other vegetables to Francis Wyatt, the governor of Virginia, at Jamestown.

1719
New Hampshire farmer

The first permanent North American potato patches were established in New England, probably near Londonderry, New Hampshire, by Scotch-Irish immigrants.

1737–1813
Antoine Auguste Parmentier

The first Frenchman to explore proper potato cultivation and to prove that the potato was a safe, nutritious food. He was enthusiastic about potato dough, which he baked into bread and distributed to the poor. His name lives on today in *potage Parmentier,* a rich, creamy soup that unites potatoes with assorted vegetables.

1790
Benjamin Thompson

An American scientist who left the colonies during the Revolution because he remained loyal to the English king, Thompson popularized the potato in Germany. A man of many talents, he became military advisor to the Duke of Bavaria.

In order to encourage greater consumption of what he considered the most nutritious vegetable, Thompson ordered each of the duke's soldiers to plant a patch of potatoes and eat the harvest.

The soldiers returned to their own farms after the fighting was finished and planted the potatoes they carried home with them. The potato had won them over. Thompson also introduced soup kitchens for the poor to Bavaria. His soup recipe is rich in spuds.

1837
Collinet

Pommes de Terre Soufflées, or puffed potatoes, were created by this legendary French chef for the king of France, Louis Philippe. The dish started out to be fried potatoes. But the king was late to arrive for the meal. The chef set the already-fried potatoes to one side and waited. Just as the king made his appearance, Collinet plunged the potatoes back into the by-now extremely hot oil in order to reheat them. To the chef's surprise the potatoes puffed up like small balloons. The king was delighted. A new recipe was born.

Puffed potatoes are the most famous of all the vegetable dishes served at Antoine's Restaurant in New Orleans.

1843
Rev. Chauncey E. Goodrich

A Protestant minister from Utica, New York, Reverend Goodrich bought some potatoes from Chile, South America, for an exorbitant sum. He devoted the next twenty years to growing at least 16,000 seedlings originating from them. His breeding work resulted in eight or ten hardy varieties, which are the ancestors of many of the potatoes grown in North America today. He derived neither fame nor fortune from his pioneering labor.

47

1845–1849
Irish famine victim

The Irish lived almost exclusively on potatoes. Wheat and grains do not grow well in rainy Ireland. Potatoes don't mind the rain as long as their feet stay dry. In the 1840s, a fungus disease appeared in potatoes, wiping out the crop. Because of their dependence on potatoes, the Irish poor had little else to eat, and millions died in the Great Famine. Thousands who were more fortunate came to the United States to live.

1870
George Crum

This chef, a Native American, is said to have invented the potato chip. It may well have been his niece, however, who made the first chip. George tasted it and, recognizing a good idea, promoted it. The potatoes were called Saratoga chips after the town in New York where George Crum worked.

1876
Luther Burbank

Burbank's fame was based on a hardy, attractive potato seedling he grew from a seed ball he stumbled upon in his mother's vegetable garden in Lancaster, Massachusetts. He promptly sold the seedling to Gregory Seed Company of Marblehead, Massachusetts, and then turned his attention to other botanical matters. From that early seedling, other plant breeders developed the variety Russet Burbank, the parent of today's most commonly grown "baking potato."

1904
Louis Lumière

A French chemist from Lyon, Lumière invented the first successful process for color photography. He used microscopic grains of potato starch fixed upon a 9-×-12-inch glass plate. These plates, or autochromes, were eventually turned out by the thousands at the Lumière factory. Autochromes were widely used until the development of color film in the 1940s.

1930s
Ora Smith

This American professor made the modern potato chip possible by devising the technology for large-scale processing. He also worked on methods of freezing potatoes for later use.

1954
Miles Willard and James Cording

These United States Department of Agriculture research scientists invented a process for making potato flakes, the basis for today's instant mashed potatoes. They carried out their work at the Eastern Regional Research Laboratory, Wyndnoor, Pennsylvania.

1950s to today
Carlos Ochoa

A Peruvian taxonomist (scientist concerned with classification of varieties), Ochoa has discovered more than forty different wild potato species in his travels throughout the Western Hemisphere.

1983
Ray Buchanan and
Ken Horne

Two ministers from Big Island, Virginia, Buchanan and Horne started the Potato Project, which distributes supposedly "waste" potatoes to those in need of food. These are potatoes rejected by the big food chains and potato processors primarily for esthetic reasons—peculiar shapes, odd blemishes, too many eyes, and other irregularities. Their nutrition is the same as that of a pretty potato. The project picks up discarded potatoes and trucks them all over the United States.

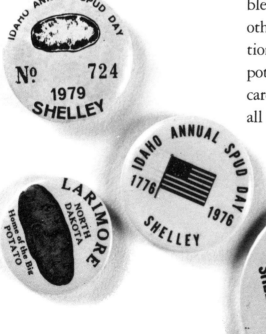

Potatoes Around

Canada
Canadian Oat Cakes — mashed potato pancakes mixed with oats and flour

USA
American Potato Chips — thin slices of potato deep-fried and eaten cold

South America
South American Cariucho — new potatoes topped with green onion and peanut butter cream sauce

MORE DELICIOUS DISHES
Australian Roast Potatoes
Indian Potato Samosas
Israeli Potato Knishes
Kenyan Iriyo
Iranian Cinnamon Potato Pie

the World

Scandinavia
Scandinavian Potatoes — boiled, served with dill (new potatoes taste best)

Northern Europe
Eastern European Pancakes — grated fresh potatoes, made into patties and fried in oil

England
English Fish and Chips — fried haddock or cod served with wedges of fried potatoes, often sprinkled with vinegar

Russia
Russian Potato Vodka — a strong, clear, alcoholic drink

eland
lcannon — potatoes d with cabbage ns

Germany
German Potato Salad — cooked cubes of potato, often served hot with a dressing

Belgium
Belgian Fries (the true "French" fry) — fresh potatoes fried twice, and served with a topping, often mayonnaise

Spain
anish Tortilla — egg — and — potato elet

Austria
Austrian Dumplings — plump potato — and — flour balls, boiled and served in beef or chicken broth

France
French Potato Soup — potatoes, butter, and cream

Switzerland
Swiss Raclette — boiled potatoes dipped with melted cheese and eaten with gherkins

Italy
Italian Gnocchi — small pieces of potato — and — flour pasta, served with tomato sauce and grated cheese

The Legend of the Potato

Long ago when the great white condor ruled the skies above the white-capped mountains of ancient Peru, the wild potato, ancestor of all the world's spuds, was first planted in the rocky, cool soil. And here is how that came to be.

Two Indian tribes lived in those mountains in uneasy togetherness. One tribe was warlike, the other peace-loving.

One day when the wind was blowing in an unfriendly direction, an erupting volcano destroyed the warriors' lands. So the warrior tribe marched on the peace lovers and made them their slaves.

Slavery did not agree with these once-happy people. One of them refused to work for the masters. Day after day he refused, and day after day he was beaten.

A god peering out from the clouds finally took

Bolivian doll dressed as an Aymara Indian

pity on the courageous man and spoke to him in a thunderous voice: "Look at the seeds I hold in my hand."

The man, though startled by the noisy god, took a peek at the seeds.

"Take these and plant them. When they grow fruit, pick them and give them to your masters to eat. But don't allow your people to try them. Wait for the leaves of the plant to die down. Then dig under the ground and eat the tasty tubers you will find there.

"Soon you will be free," the god added, drawing the clouds back around him.

The courageous man looked down at the seeds he found in the palm of his hand. "Well," he thought, "what a helpful god." And off he trotted to plant the seeds.

The rotten warrior rulers greedily devoured the delicious-looking little green berries that grew from the plants that grew from the seeds.

Then they died long, wretched deaths full of stomachache.

But the slaves, starving though they were, waited to eat the promised tubers hidden in the earth.

Then, their strength renewed with potato power, the slaves overthrew those of their rulers who remained and settled down to live happily ever after with potatoes.

Just as the god had promised, the wild potato had cleverly hidden its goodness underground and tempted the hungry passerby with its pretty but poisonous fruit.

This story was tracked down and recorded in Bolivia by an American foreign-service officer working with the Association for International Development.

THE PLAYFUL POTATO

Play around with a potato and you'll see it's not such a dull, brown blob after all. You can juggle with it, print with it, make puppets from it, toss it, carve it, dress it, even wear it. You can hang around with it, take a walk with it. Potatoes are versatile.

People laugh at potato jokes. They write and sing potato songs. They dance to potato music. They tell tall tater tales. They draw silly spud cartoons. They even call each other potato nicknames. Potatoes are friendly and comfortable. They make us feel cozy and cared for.

People and potatoes have good times together.

Like peas in a pod, fish in the sea, umbrellas in the rain, potatoes and people belong.

Potato-face toy of the 1940s

One Potato, Two Potato . . .

Many of you are familiar with the rhyme that goes "One potato, two potato, three potato, four, five potato, six potato, seven potato, MORE!" Here's a choosing-up rhyme from Scotland that you may not know.

"Three small tatties in a pot. Take one out and see if it's hot. If it's hot, cut its throat. Two small tatties in a pot." And so on.

You use it the same way as one potato. Everyone in the game holds out two fists and one person called in England the "spudder" or "potato masher" starts the count.

Pick Up Chips—
A Game You'll Eat Up

Similar to pick up sticks or jackstraws, this game involves your favorite brand of potato chip. Toss the contents of a small bag onto a table. The idea is to remove as many chips as you can without bringing down the whole mound. Keep track of those you remove safely. The player with the most wins, in more ways than one. At the end of the game all the contestants eat up their chips.

Sack Racing

Team Taters

Get your friends together and choose up two teams. Each side gets one tablespoon and one potato. The two teams line up next to each other, players in single file. The first players in each line place a potato on the spoon, put one hand behind their backs, and run down the field and back, trying to keep the spud on the spoon. The team that finishes first wins, of course.

Musical Spuds

This is similar to musical chairs. Sit in a circle, start the music, and hand a potato around. Remember it's a "hot potato," so you want to get rid of it as fast as you can. When the music stops, the player holding the spud is out. The game continues until only one person, the winner, is left.

Here's a tater mouthful to use the next time you jump rope with your friends.

POTATOES

Potatoes on the table,
  to eat with other things.
Potatoes with their jackets off
  may do for Dukes and Kings;
But if you wish to taste them
  as nature meant you should,
Be sure to keep their jackets on
  and eat them in the wood.

—Edward Verrall Lucas

Short and Sassy Rope Rhyme

How are your potatoes?
—Very small.
How do you eat them?
—Skins and all.
—Folk song
New Brunswick, Canada

Celebrate the Potato

Children at Wheeler Avenue School in Long Island, New York, celebrate "Mickey Day" every year in the late spring. Every child brings a potato to school. The teacher helps the child carve his or her initials into the spud. Then the spuds are thrown into an outdoor oven constructed for the day by teachers and kids. The baked potatoes are eaten for lunch. In the old days the children brought potatoes to school regularly and roasted them in a wood-burning stove. Mickey, in case you hadn't guessed it, is a nickname for the potato.

You can run in a fifteen-kilometer potato stomp, enter a potato-chip contest, taste goodies in the potato baking competition, even watch contestants wrestle in mounds of instant mashed potatoes. Where? At the Mantua, Ohio, potato festival, held every September.

Sporting Potatoes

Luke "Hot Potato" Hamlin—A twenty-game winner in 1939 with the Brooklyn Dodgers, Hamlin was nicknamed by a New York sports writer who noticed him tossing two baseballs in the air as he warmed up to pitch.

Virgil "Spud" Davis—A catcher for the St. Louis Cardinals in the 1930s, Davis averaged .330 at the plate in one six-year period. Davis once said his cousin called him Spud after observing his single-minded devotion to his favorite food.

Howard "Spud" Krist—Another Cardinal in the 1930s, this right-handed reliever favored potatoes on his father's farm in New York.

VIRGIL DAVIS

LUKE "HOT POTATO" HAMLIN

Spurgeon "Spud" Chandler—A New Jersey
sports writer decided Spurgeon was an inappro-
priate name for this capable Yankee pitcher of the
1930s and 1940s. Spud he became and Spud he
remained. Evidently he liked the idea.

. . . .

A baseball is sometimes called "the potato."

. . . .

A Richmond, Virginia, high-school catcher
made the "potato hat-trick play" famous. It
seems the runner was leading off third, ready to
come home. The pitcher tossed the ball to the
catcher, who came up with it as if to throw over
to third. The runner started back to third, and
saw what he thought was the ball sailing past the
base. He turned for home and was tagged out at
the plate by the catcher.

How? The catcher had lobbed a potato past
third base. The baseball was safely in his glove
the whole time. The umpires were not amused.

. . . .

High fliers in Clines Corners, New Mexico,
own and operate a hot-air balloon called the
"Spud."

Play on Your Tater Bug

The potato-bug mandolin is a round-backed, four- or six-string, strummable instrument. It usually has a yellow-and-black-striped wood back, resembling the body of the Colorado potato beetle. So, it's easy to see how the mandolin acquired its name in the United States. The instrument came originally from Italy.

Did You Know . . that two dozen festivals in North America are dedicated to the potato?

. . that instant mashed-potato flakes have been used by Hollywood moviemakers to simulate fallen snow?

Question: In what movie did mashed potatoes play a key role?

Answer: *Close Encounters of the Third Kind.* The hero comes close to discovering the location of the extraterrestrials' secret landing site when he sculpts a mountain of mashies on his dinner plate.

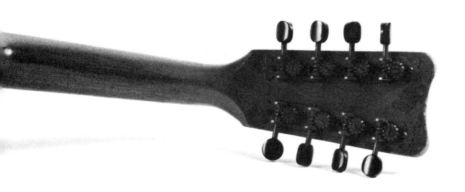

More Musical Potatoes

Put on your dancing spuds and do:

the Potato Peelings Polka
the Mashed Potato
the Hot Potato Mambo
the Potato Bug Boogie

Sing a Song of Spuds

Oh! potatoes they grow small over there!

Oh! potatoes they grow small over there!

Oh! potatoes they grow small

Cause they plant 'em in the fall

And then eats 'em tops and all

Over there.

(To the tune of "They'll Be Comin' Round the Mountain")
—*New Singer's Journal #23*

The "over there" in the song refers to Ireland. Desperately poor people there, unfamiliar with the potato when it was first planted, may have eaten every bit of the plant.

Tater Tall Tale

"You say you want twenty-five pounds of potatoes?" asked the grocer of his new customer.

The customer smiled and nodded.

"Well, you must be a stranger in these parts, because everybody around here knows we don't cut a potato in two for *anybody*!"

Potato People

- A Canadian theater group called Potato People wears white masks and performs in mime. Their characters' names are Poppa Potato, Mama Potato, and so on.

- A fellow named Herb and his partner known as Potato do comedy routines in New York City.

- "His pet name for me was Potato," said actress Lillian Gish of one of her admirers.

- "I was born an Idaho potato," said artist Ray Johnson of himself.

- Mr. Potato Head was the first toy to be advertised on American television.